Click Into Lead

Aaron Opfell

CONTENTS

PREFACE

Ever since I was eight years old and wandering around the public library holding an Isaac Asimov novel, I've wanted to write a book. Perhaps it is natural that this work is nonfiction rather than the novel I always imagined writing, as online advertising has been my all-consuming focus for the past several years.

But it's still strange to me that I would write a book about online advertising and lead generation. Hasn't that topic been covered? To my surprise, not in an updated, complete, and unbiased way. Everything I read and researched on the topic favored one type of advertising over another, or confused marketing and advertising, or was out-of-date, missed key concepts, or was overly self-promotional. Taking stock of this, I felt there was room for some of my opinions—ideas and concepts born from my experience. Therefore, in a process that has spanned over two years, I have finally collected into this work a complete, if high-level, view of the combination of tactics that are required for success in lead generation in today's digital landscape.

The main challenge with writing a comprehensive book about online advertising and lead generation is the sheer volume of information regarding methods and services. There are, for example, over 200 publicly traded companies offering digital advertising services. The big fish such as Google and Facebook would have you believe that their offering is the one true solution for you. Journalists and bloggers take the facts and spin, slant, slice. Most of the information provided online has bias; some content actively pushes towards a specific solution or vendor. Writing articles related to your services is very effective marketing, and in later chapters, I'll talk about how you can do that exact thing with your company. Since all news and blogs (and even forums!) do this, it's near impossible to separate fact from recycled fiction in the online advertising biz, and that's why I wrote this book.

When I started, my goal was to write a single book that could cover the entire life cycle of lead generation: an overview of traffic into leads into sales. After over a year of writing, I realized that traffic into leads and leads into sales were actually completely different processes or "funnels," however interrelated, and beyond the scope of one book. I decided to separately publish the material I had written about generating traffic and leads with online marketing and advertising. Turning leads into revenue is a critically important process, and it will be covered in a separate work. In this book, I'm going to share with you everything I know about internet advertising and marketing techniques for lead generation: how to generate the right type of leads—real, verified contacts that are genuinely interested in your company and service, leads that close.

If you own or operate a service-based business that buys or generates leads, I want you to finish this book and walk away feeling richer for the experience. I welcome feedback; email me at info@clickintolead.com. Let's be clear, this book is one of my methods of lead generation. Rest assured I am A/B testing, so if you don't convert now—catch you next edition!

Onwards & Upwards,

Aaron Opfell

ACKNOWLEDGMENTS

A huge shout-out to all my friends and colleagues who gave their time and support, without whom this book would have never been but a to-do item due "later."

- Shane Barker, for that interview on social marketing and for much beer-fueled brainstorming

- Eric Iffland, for an interview on landing page design (in the next book)

- Christopher Minnick, for his mentorship of struggling authors and for lending his minnickificent brain

- Erin Kwok, for her graphic design skills and for the cover art and typesetting of this book

- The rest of the SearcherMag.net team, for

delivering results to our clients that are worth writing about, and for being telepathic

- Steve Simonetto, the best damn sounding board ever, and for being Columbo

- Gina Lujan, for constant encouragement, positivity, and "grassroots disruptive innovation" (AKA getting into trouble)

- All the bad books I've read that convinced me I could write something better

- The Almighty Google, for creating the industry that feeds my family

- My mother, for cursing me with a lifelong appreciation for literature, and for criticizing me where it counted

- My father, for demanding my best effort, and being patient with college dropouts

ACRONYMS

AIDA attention, interest, decision, action

B2B business-to-business

B2C business-to-consumer

CMO chief marketing officer

CPA cost per acquisition

CPC cost per click

CPM cost per thousand (impressions, not clicks)

CPS cost per sent email

CPV cost per view

CTR click-through rate (ad impressions vs. clicks)

DMP data management platform

ERP enterprise resource planning

FBX Facebook Exchange

GDN Google Display Network

KPI key performance indicator

OS operating system

POS point of sale

PPC pay per click

ROI return on investment

SEM search engine marketing

SEO search engine optimization

URL uniform resource locator, or website address

INTRODUCTION

Click Into Lead is about lead-generation strategies for people who are already motivated. This book can't help people who aren't ready for it.

There are three types of people who should not read this book.

First are the decision makers who do not want to grow their business. People who are happy with their current revenue and sales, stop reading here.

Second are those who believe that there is only one method to generate leads for their industry that works. Yes, testing new advertising and marketing has risk, and it's safe to repeat a sure thing. But nothing ventured, nothing gained—how can anyone be sure there's no better return on investment (ROI) without testing new things?

Third are people who insist that internet lead generation doesn't work for their business. Right now their competitors are engaging with prospective customers and are actively investing in and ramping up digital strategies. This book provides an overview of internet lead generation that can be utilized by anyone or any company aiming to develop lead generation and an online presence, but to get the most value out of it readers need to be willing to challenge their assumptions.

Chapter 2 defines what a lead is and the deals that get made by lead brokers and data aggregators. Next, Chapters 3 and 4 examine common failure points in lead-generation campaigns and why traditional media response rates are dropping like a rock. Then Chapter 5 explains the difference between branding and direct-response advertising. Only after setting the foundation of modern lead generation do later chapters look at the most specific and highest ROI techniques ranging from the use of search engine optimization (SEO), search engine marketing (SEM), retargeting, email marketing, affiliate marketing, social media, and display ads. From this viewpoint, it is possible to get a comprehensive look at all the channels modern marketers and advertisers use to generate leads on today's internet. Ultimately, the reader should walk away with not only new strategies to test but also a better holistic understanding of something known as multichannel or omnichannel marketing.

Details aside, the mission of this book is to clearly and concisely communicate the most effective lead-generation techniques available online. One of the biggest barriers to learning online advertising and marketing is the industry jargon and terminology. It's hard to describe the landscape without using ugly acronyms like CTR, CPC, PPC—and it's OK to look up what they mean. They often have different meanings in different contexts. Even experts will frequently mix them up. Many are synonyms of each other, and meanings change. Readers shouldn't get hung up on terms—if something is unfamiliar, by all means look it up, highlight it, underline it, insert a Post-it note, or dog-ear the page. This book is meant to be used as a reference manual. Understanding these concepts isn't easy, and further explanation can be found on http://www.clickintolead.com, the author's company website www.searchermag.net/blog, Google, or Wikipedia.

This book is information-dense. It is not a fluff self-promotional marketing piece. It contains facts and experiences developed over nearly a decade, true insider secrets that can be directly applied to any lead-generation campaign. While it's possible to read it straight through, cover to cover, that's not necessary. It's recommended that readers look at the table of contents. What's the most interesting chapter at this exact second? Read that chapter first. This book will have the most value where it closely aligns to the reader's current business needs.

THE DEFINITION OF "LEAD"

What is a lead? Whatever a particular company defines it to be. The term *lead* is shorthand for "sales lead." One commonly accepted definition is "a person or company interested in purchasing a product or service." But every industry has a slightly different opinion of what a lead is and what it's called. Real estate agents call leads "prospects." Business-to-business (B2B) companies often call them "contacts." Lead generation is quite simply the act of creating these opportunities. Industry jargon aside, there are a few objective criteria to use when defining what is a lead and what is instead just data. The biggest lead-generation companies define a lead to be real-time, validated, qualified, and having purchasing intent. This book will refer to these and other standards as the Golden Lead Generation Rule. Real-time leads are delivered to a company's sales force as they are generated. Validated leads have contact information that is correct (or as accurate as possible). Qualified leads are truly interested in a product or service, and they haven't been generated under false pretenses. Leads must also intend to make a purchase (or will influence the purchase decision). This book discusses how to execute these four criteria and more when generating leads online.

Despite what may be advertised, cold data is usually not a lead. There are thousands of companies, called list brokers, that sell lists of names generated from a database. Because these lists are not generated in real time, they fail the Golden Lead Generation Rule. Lists are not leads! Lists can be an amazingly effective way to generate leads, but they are not in themselves leads. List brokers usually sell cold data. These lists contain public record data that loosely match the specified data, or filters, that the list buyer selected. Do not be deceived by claims that these filters are targeted leads; they are usually no more selective than the telephone directory white pages. A common red flag is an absurdly low price per record, such as twenty-five cents or one dollar. (A record is the related data about one lead, such as name and phone number.) This low pricing guarantees that what's being sold is actually a list, not leads.

One warmer variation on cold data is the lucrative "trigger leads" industry: ultraspecific (and expensive) data sold by credit bureaus or data warehouses. This questionable practice provides the end lead buyer with the names, addresses, emails and often cell phone numbers of consumers who have, for example, mortgage-related credit inquiries on their credit report indicating a recent loan application, and thus an opening for a second opinion.

Any sales staff who attempt to dial through the names and numbers on such a purchased list will be met with the full rejection of a cold call because the people on this list have no clue about the caller's company. Through the use of heavy marketing campaigns via email, postal mail, or predictive autodialers, a well-targeted list can be converted into leads, but this process is not without time, effort, and expense. Unfortunately, though contacting the names one by one is the cheapest way of reaching out to a purchased list, it's the most demoralizing and time-consuming method for salespeople.

A close cousin to the list broker is the lead broker. A lead broker exists solely for the purpose of brokering or vending leads. If they also sell lists, these lists are either (a) cold data, sourced from one of the big databases, or (b) aged leads, data that has already been sold at least once. The lead broker game is one of arbitrage, or buy low, sell high. Leads are almost never produced in-house; they are almost always aggregated from a vast array of sources, including other brokers. Since the broker makes money on the difference between the lead cost and the sales price, the game is rigged if the buyer doesn't know the value or quality of the lead. It's important to note that the lead broker usually has little interest in the media and marketing message used to generate the lead, with most of the broker's focus on cost. Reputable lead brokers will offer returns for leads that fail validation or do not qualify, and they are interested in repeat business.

A relationship with a lead broker, especially one who specializes in a niche or high volume, can sometimes be profitable. However, because they do not have full control of their sources, the volume and quality can vary wildly—putting the lead buyer's profit at risk.

Lead brokers will sometimes claim to have exclusive leads. This is essentially an unverifiable claim. When purchasing leads from a broker, there is zero guarantee of exclusivity. Lead brokers know that most lead buyers don't work the lead properly, wasting its value and opening opportunities for others. To stay competitive on price, lead brokers typically sell leads about three to seven times to extract maximum profit. Because of natural human tendencies in both the buyer (inefficiency in aggressively contacting the lead) and the lead (delay and hesitation in the buying cycle), the broker-buyer is most profitable when a single lead is sold to multiple buyers. This is just an unfortunate reality of the business. A small percentage of brokers do honor their exclusive guarantee—but only for as little as a few days, and then the leads are resold. After thirty to sixty days, lead brokers repackage old leads as "aged data" to a list provider. Often lead brokers operate a list business or have a partner company that manages lists. Any leads they have in inventory usually end up in these lists. In the best case these extra leads are for complementary products (for instance, adding old mortgage leads to a credit repair list).

In the case of aged data, as long as 30, 60, 90, or even 180 days following the initial sale, it's very common for competitors to purchase the old leads at a sharply reduced price. Though legally permissible, this practice is ethically questionable, and almost never disclosed to the end buyer. As they are now "warm leads," this competitor will employ high-impact marketing such as direct mail, autodialers, and bulk email marketing to cherry-pick deals right out of the original buyer's sales pipeline. When direct competitors magically seem to know right when to contact a company's new clients, resale has happened.

Profit often pits the lead broker against lead purchasers. As mentioned previously, lead brokers know that most buyers are sloppy about follow-up, so they comfortably resell leads. But there are other tricks of the trade to be on the lookout for. After the buyer makes an initial test order, lead brokers will sometimes salt the next purchase with aged leads to get their cost down and profit up. Or, if leads are being driven by a particular media—for example, leads generated from pay per click (PPC)—they may mix in lower quality traffic leads from sub-prime sources. This salting will not be enough to ruin the buyer's campaign, just enough to pad the lead broker's profit margin. As leads purchasers have no oversight into the campaign that generated the leads, it's impossible to determine when this is happening. Buyers should ask to see the advertisements and actual websites that generated the leads and negotiate a return policy in the contract. When the purchase is delivered, buyers must be watchful for changes in lead quality, and include a "who else has contacted you" question as part of the sales script. The contact ratio needs to be continually monitored, and the sales team needs to provide feedback periodically. Keeping an eye on lead generation can help buyers stay ahead of the game.

The one true benefit to working with lead brokers is economy of scale. If buyers are willing to pay market price for leads, the broker can negotiate with the aggregators. By the nature of their business, brokers form a huge network of niche suppliers, affiliates, resellers, and other vendors. They have massive leverage across their network if the price is right. Ultimately, lead brokers only care about price per lead and volume. If a buyer can place an order with high volume and a large sticker price, a most curious thing will happen: the lead broker will do backflips to make the buyer happy. Brokers cannot profit on little orders except by charging a huge margin. With a big order volume, the lead broker achieves economy of scale. A fair exchange is passing the savings on to the buyer in the form of reduced prices. Buyers should have an open discussion about what kind of volume discount is available and even a guarantee on the buyer's part of increased order volume. Transparency is mutually profitable—especially if buyers can show the lead broker that their sales team is rock solid and can handle any leads they buy.

What is the purpose of this in-depth look at list and

lead brokers? Most businesses focus on these sources because they are the most common way to get leads. However, for the reasons outlined above, most leads sold through these channels fail to serve the purchaser well.

BUT WHAT MAKES FOR AN EXCELLENT LEAD?

Here are the six characteristics that comprise the Golden Lead Generation Rule:

- **Exclusive:** Leads should have a 1:1 exclusivity with the buyer's sales team.

- **Real Time:** Leads should be delivered and worked as generated.

- **Validated:** Leads should have accurate (non-fake) contact info.

- **Contextual:** Advertising collateral such as ads and websites should truly represent the value of the product or service.

- **Transparent:** The marketing message on the landing page or content should be genuine and clearly communicate to the prospect what they are signing up for.

- **Intent:** The leads should be able and willing to make or influence a purchase.

It's simply impossible to execute all of these when purchasing leads. A superior alternative is generating leads in-house, which will be discussed in depth over the course of this book. Following these guidelines closely is the guaranteed path to increasing performance and ROI. Generating leads online is not unlike making a cake—use one low-quality ingredient, and the result can fall flat.

COMPANIES ARE DOING LEAD GENERATION WRONG

Many business owners or CMOs will flatly state that it's impossible to generate leads online. They complain about cost or complexity, or say that their audience is "not online." The last item is completely false: as of the fourth quarter of 2012, more than 273 million households, or 78% of the North American population, were online.[i] Choosing not to engage in online lead generation is often justified by citing a previous bad experience. Lead generation involves lots of moving parts and failure points, with the top mistake being a failure to effectively leverage existing assets. Many businesses have tons of web assets that are underutilized. Common problems affecting lead generation include

- Hiding price lists, processes, and data sheets behind firewalls

- Abandoning websites, domain names, or social media properties

- Out-of-date or abandoned SEM accounts, social profiles, and blogs

- Unsuitable-for-audience copy or design

- Marketing messages and promotions that lack continuity

PAID MEDIA PROBLEMS

For paid or organic media on properties such as

Google, Bing, Facebook, and Twitter, the problem with internal efforts goes deeper. For a social, SEO, or SEM campaign to have any possibility of success, a well-built and -maintained keyword profile is critical. Keywords are the terms and hash tags prospective clients search for, so it's vital that advertising be closely aligned with them. Keyword portfolios cannot be "set and forget"; they must be regularly updated to reflect changing user search behavior. Pruning keywords takes effort, and a good start is to remove

- Keywords that don't match buyers' search behavior

- Keywords that don't have traffic volume

- Keywords with low-quality scores

- Keywords that don't convert

- Keywords that drive the wrong customer

- Keywords that cost too much

- Keywords that are overly competitive

If it's hard to make decisions due to lack of conversion data, it might be time to reevaluate how paid media spends against lead-generation goals are measured.

ATTENTION, INTEREST, DECISION, ACTION

Even with a healthy "top-of-funnel" paid or organic media campaign, it's all too common for the conversion path to be outdated or ineffective. For lead generation to work correctly, all parts must work together in a system. A fantastic illustration of this concept, AIDA, is shown in the award-winning play (and later movie) *Glengarry Glen Ross*. Addressing a group of real estate salesmen (played by a young Al Pacino and Jack Lemmon, among others), Alec Baldwin takes them through Attention, Interest, Decision, and Action—the four classic components of the sales cycle.

The AIDA concept is easily extended to other areas and specifically to online advertising and lead generation, as shown below:

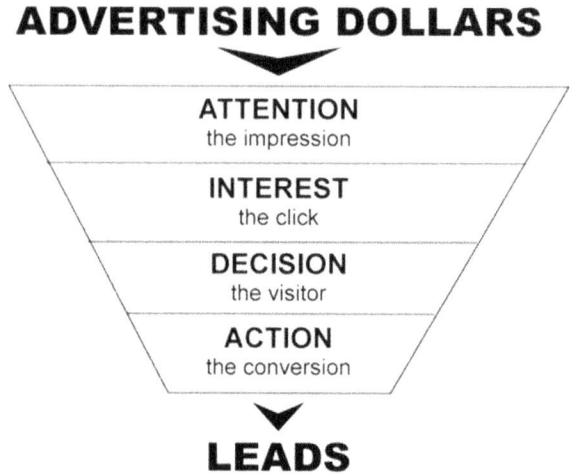

ADVERTISING DOLLARS

ATTENTION
the impression

INTEREST
the click

DECISION
the visitor

ACTION
the conversion

LEADS

Although a lead-generation funnel may run like a well-tuned Ferrari, the generated leads might not translate well into sales. In larger companies, or for those with complex sales cycles, tracking lead conversion is difficult to even contemplate, let alone manage. This is because once a lead is generated, it enters another system—the sales funnel.

The sales funnel operates in a similar way as AIDA:

SALES FAILS

Common failure points in a sales funnel include

- No definition of "lead"

- Not tracking contact rate and conversion rate across lead sources

- No or limited ability to track and measure

sales performance

- No formal follow-up or lead nurturing process

- Making less than three contact attempts on average

- Response time during business hours is over five minutes for consumers or over one hour for businesses

- Lack of email marketing (prewritten messages sent at specific points)

- Not having anyone in a sales manager role

These are just a few areas where sales funnels can break. Later chapters dig deeper into the sales funnel with actionable advice about lead nurturing, lead tracking, sales management, and related strategies.

TRADITIONAL MEDIA IS DOING LEAD GENERATION WRONG

As the old song title goes, "The Times They Are a-Changin'." As of just 2011, the online advertising market hit $72.18 billion.[ii] Since its introduction in the '90s, online advertising has been the only form of advertising to post year-over-year growth, with every other form of advertising (radio, classifieds, print) except television declining. Yet even the advertising giant of TV is rapidly evolving under heavy pressure from the internet. Increasingly, many young people consume their TV programming online through web services like Hulu and YouTube, or through new hardware like Boxee, Roku, and TV tuner cards.[iii] Over the last three years, Nielsen reported the following declines in weekly TV viewing in younger age groups:

- Age 18–24 watched 4 hours less TV

- Age 25–34 watched 2.5 hours less TV

- Age 35–49 watched 2.75 hours less TV

Though Netflix is no doubt responsible for the lion's share of the decline of cable and network TV viewing in younger demographics, BitTorrent shares responsibility. BitTorrent allows easy piracy of just about any video content and avoids the insertion of advertiser messages entirely. TV shows distributed via BitTorrent commonly have all ads and even watermarks edited out by diligent (and apparently highly quality-conscious) uploaders. Copyright law is outside the scope of this work, but some credit is due to services such as Spotify, which entered the streaming music business under the slogan "an alternative to music piracy."[iv] Services such as Spotify and Pandora have made a measurable dent in music piracy by making the experience low-cost and effortless from a consumer perspective. Services like Google TV, Netflix, and Hulu are starting to make similar moves, and the trend will continue through all forms of media—the *Wall Street Journal* has experimented with online paywalls since 1995.[v]

MOBILE MATTERS

As of this writing, 4.3 million people have viewed the video of the baby unsuccessfully trying to swipe a magazine as if it were an iPad.[vi] The United States is seeing rapid and widespread adoption of mobile devices and a growing reliance on use in daily life.

Many US schools are equipping kindergarten classes with iPads, and Grandpa is texting on his iPhone. Especially interesting is mobile use by culture and ethnicity: Hispanic markets have the highest smartphone use rate. Tablet sales, fueled by low-cost Android devices, are exploding into the Baby Boomer generation as the "third screen," not as full-featured as a desktop computer, but more convenient for content consumption than a phone. Older generations are realizing their favorite newspapers and magazines can be had instantly in the palm of their hand instead of slowly arriving at the front door. A recent study concluded that one-third of all tablet buyers are over the age of 45,[vii] and 18% of those aged 65 owned a smart phone![viii] What are these seniors doing with these devices? Not playing games, as the 18–29 year old demographic is. Instead, seniors spend over half their tablet time on email, videos, and ebooks.

ANALOG SIGNALS GETTING STATIC

For larger brands or companies that run integrated media across both traditional and digital channels, the question is always attribution. And answering it is a doozy. Say Target is running a billboard, a radio ad, and an AdWords downloadable coupon campaign in one zip code. The consumer experiences all three, but downloads the coupon right before buying. Which media channel gets credit for that sale? How did the radio ad influence or assist the sale? Ability to measure these interactions is slowly shaping up in tools like Google's Universal Analytics, software that attempts to answer modern marketing's multibillion dollar question: What is the trackable, measurable, quantifiable impact of multichannel marketing?

The internet advertising industry's struggles with the offline world are mild in comparison to the problems and missed opportunities faced by other industries.

Restaurants and Retail: Businesses making in-person sales are often stuck with "dumb" cash registers that don't connect to the internet in a meaningful way. The point-of-sale software industry, which somewhat ironically uses the acronym POS, is infamous for locking businesses into a walled garden. It is incredibly difficult for brick-and-mortar businesses to employ loyalty cards, rewards programs, and cloud inventory solutions or customer-related software innovation without making massive investments in customizing their existing POS hardware or merchant processing. Kudos to companies like Square, PayPal, and Vend for revolutionizing POS for small merchants. For enterprise solutions, the industry is stuck in the world of long and complicated enterprise resource planning (ERP) and costly custom programmed solutions.

Customer Databases: Many business-to-consumer (B2C) companies fail to properly leverage customer databases with email, mail, or retargeting internet ads. When first collecting email addresses, many companies that don't have automated processes wait days or months before opting-in leads into an email database. Emails that aren't automatically subscribed to a high-quality, regular newsletter lose about 80% of potential response rate. Email lists colder than six months are lucky to get above a 0.25% response rate. Technology is now fully available to push customer data in real time to a specialized mail house, allowing fully personalized mail pieces to be automatically sent—a technique few take advantage of. Perhaps the most highly targeted form of database leverage is the use of retargeting—the process of matching a database with online ad targets, allowing delivery of specific ad messages across every stage of the buyer cycle.

Traditional Advertising: Every time a TV, radio, and print ad is run without a digital call to action, an opportunity for sales is missed. Due to lack of technical skills, traditional ad agencies often omit URLs from their ads, and lose extra traffic and sales that could be generated online. The use of a QR code (a barcode readable by most mobile phones) allows users to instantly download an app or view mobile content, yet print media is slow to adopt these calls to action. In recent years, a trend has developed, especially in Super Bowl commercials, to include a social media URL in the ad to promote the brand's Facebook or Twitter page. Large companies have realized that social media conversations are "top of funnel," providing a less threatening and more engaging first impression than a website or landing page.

Traditional Marketing: Response rates to

telemarketing and mass direct-mail campaigns are dropping like a rock. Telemarketing, under legal duress by ever-stricter compliance law, finds a new hurdle in the Google Voice spam project,[ix] an automatic database that allows users to block any commercial caller, similar to the spam system for the popular Gmail service. It is now common behavior to let unknown numbers go to voicemail, and many web services such as WhoCalled.us allow a fast and accurate lookup of the company behind the call. Direct mail has been plagued with response rate problems, with letter-sized direct mail response rates dropping 25% over a nine-year period.[x] Unless ultraspecifically targeted, direct mail is a complete failure in the under-30 demographic, whose members sign up for e-bills, tend not to write or receive letters, and view checking the mail as a chore.

TAKEAWAY

Plain and simple, the old ways of lead generation are broken, and so are the approaches of many marketing firms and ad agencies. If a company's lead and sales funnels are unclear or the methods used to drive traffic to them are outdated, it could be time to make some changes.

THE DIFFERENCE BETWEEN BRANDING AND DIRECT RESPONSE

IF YOU BUILD IT, THEY MIGHT COME

Everyone agrees that businesses need a website, if for no reason other than branding and professional credibility. It is all too common, however, to launch a brand-new website and have the phone be deathly silent. The fact is that websites without internet marketing or advertising are all but guaranteed to have NO LEADS. It's certainly possible to get visitors through internal efforts such as business cards, Craigslist, and social media, but these methods don't scale well or gain momentum. Thus, many businesses find themselves forced to continue investing time and money in self-promotional efforts indefinitely.

BUT MY WEB DESIGNER SAID . . .

A logo and website don't do much by themselves, though a web designer might advise differently. It's true that a company's online brand is the gateway for internet advertising and marketing. However, web designers, whether freelancers or those on payroll, are almost never trained in promotions, and so the website functions as a brand, as opposed to being a true lead-generation funnel. One of the most important considerations when designing a website is SEO, and unfortunately most websites launch without any consideration in that area. Why does this happen?

- Any good web designer is usually a very right-brain, creative-vision type person. Since SEO is a very technical and repetitive left-brain task, web designers won't find it easy or fun.

- Web designers and programmers not trained in SEO will often distance themselves from it, viewing it as extra work. They also avoid the additional responsibility of implementing SEO, which impacts most areas of the website.

- Some years ago, web designers were the gateway to the internet, and they bundled SEO, hosting, and other services. Now specialists such as social media/SEO consultants, developers, and advertising agencies are needed for a holistic online presence, forcing web designers to give up their status as the sole go-to internet expert.

About five years ago, it was possible to dump a handful of keywords on a page and get SEO results. But with the recent Google algorithm changes and increased online competition, it takes a team with a diverse skill set to achieve the best results. Yet sole web designers may insist that they can still deliver adequate SEO for a company that needs to replace the traditional advertising that is no longer effective.

The biggest SEO killers are Flash or poorly implemented scripting. SEO-invisible sites often get built because the web designer felt it was the only way to meet the client's taste and either didn't know or failed to disclose the SEO consequences. In more complex platforms like Joomla and WordPress, changes that seem minor from the designer's perspective can have catastrophic effects on SEO.

While it is common to find web designers who "know SEO," finding one who also knows internet advertising is like finding a unicorn. Search concepts and messages should drive web design, not be tacked on as an afterthought. If the website is large or when dealing with tight brand guidelines, consider the use of nonbranded or separate landing pages to stay "brand safe" while allowing for maximum marketing ROI.

BUT MY AD AGENCY SAID . . .

When an ad agency talks about "exposure" and "raising awareness," they are selling branding, not lead generation. There is a huge difference between branding and direct response advertising messages. Branding gets a company's name out there. Direct response generates leads. Companies should ask what type of advertising their agency specializes in.

Here's a chart to clarify the differences between the two types of advertising:

	Branding	Direct Response
Goal	Excite People	Motivate People
Message	We're Awesome	We're A Solution
Call to Action	Vague or Missing	Act Now!
Vibe	Feel Good	Buy Now!
Measurable	Rarely	Always
Results	Name Recognition	Leads and Sales

The phrase "direct response" brings to mind late night infomercials and obnoxious sales letters. Although these tactics are very effective for certain products, they are definitely not appropriate for every brand. What many ad agencies miss when focusing exclusively on the branding method is the opportunity to drive measurable outcomes. Brand advertising often works for multimillion-dollar brands and budgets, but some businesses have more tactical needs. With the right creative team, it's possible to run highly effective direct response internet campaigns that not only maintain brand integrity but also enhance it.

SEO BEST PRACTICES

SEO is a powerful lead-generation tactic, although unpredictable if executed incorrectly. To see the rapid transformation that is happening in SEO, start by examining search engines circa 2005. In those simpler times, it was possible for marketers to rank websites in organic search—even for very competitive terms—by doing no more than a little keyword stuffing and link farming. Google took notice, even though it could do little about it at the time, and over the years Google has feverishly updated their algorithm to include over 1,000 different factors in its ranking, pushing out major updates like Panda and Penguin that cut traffic from millions of websites. How a business views SEO should depend on whether the web presence is new or established. New web presences should focus on creating high-quality content while established sites should also make sure their existing assets aren't being penalized in organic search results. Either way, effective SEO comes only from holistic, unique content that reinforces a company's brand and provides real value to its audience. SEO must be connected to all parts of lead-generation and sales funnels to be really effective.

HOW SEO WORKS

Any business with an in-house marketing team knows that good SEO comes from a large time investment. For most established businesses, it's easily equivalent to a full-time employee. Naturally, many companies turn to outsourcing, but they have trouble sorting through the smoke and mirrors of the SEO industry. A great example of an unscrupulous SEO tactic is "top of Google," when salespeople guarantee first-position rankings for keywords but are actually selling first-place-position ads in Google AdWords. The buyers have no idea that they are paying for paid placement, not marketing efforts, but they are content paying the monthly fees because their ads are "top of Google." It's unfortunate, but many brands focus solely on the ranking aspect of SEO and ignore the lead-generation aspect by failing to track and attribute conversions to the source. A legitimate SEO firm will thoroughly audit a business web presence and plan a campaign over months or years to address both on-site and off-site marketing objectives.

WHY GOOGLE CARES ABOUT QUALITY

Google's business model is to charge advertisers for the privilege of appearing above search results. Google must maintain a high-quality user experience or risk losing search volume to competitors like Bing and Yahoo. A delicate balance is maintained between paid and organic content. Time and time again, Google's engineers make changes to search results pages that favor user engagement, usually uncaring or ignorant of the effect on individual websites. For years, Google has been introducing rich content (either media like video or images, or enhanced search results). Examples include:

- **March Madness and sports scores**—to the detriment of ESPN.com and other sites

- **Airfare and trip data**—to the detriment of Priceline.com and travel sites

- **Google Maps and Google+**—to the detriment of local organically ranked businesses

- **Weather, news, events, concert tickets, mortgage rates, etc.**—to the detriment of the sites producing the information that Google shows on the results page

Furthermore, Google is continually rebuilding its search algorithm, up to 600 times per year,[xi] to prevent website owners from gaming it. The Panda update alone affected 3% of all search queries in the United States.[xii] What worked a few years or even a few months ago could now be deeply toxic, poisoning rankings with an unnatural link penalty.

LINKS TO LEADS: BUILDING CITATIONS WITH SEO

The famous PageRank algorithm dictates that the rank of any given web page is based on the links that point to it. With Google's recent Panda and Penguin updates, link portfolios became critically important. Once a free-for-all, the portfolio of links pointing to a site became subject to intense scrutiny. In today's organic search game, a business is all but guaranteed to be penalized if any of its portfolio links have these characteristics:

- Low variance in anchor text (many exactly match keyword links)

- Links sourced from low-quality or spammy sites

- Lack of diversity in link sources

- Lack of diversity in link URLs (all links point to home page)

THE POWER OF THE PRESS

Another popular spray-and-pray SEO link-building technique is the press release. Today's press release websites are subject to the same quality guidelines that affect article directories. Additionally, search engines take a dim view of links contained within press releases, requiring that the "rel=nofollow" attribute (essentially removing value from the link) be added to these types of links. According to

Google, "links with optimized anchor text in articles or press releases distributed on other sites"[xiii] violate their guidelines, judging the content to be an advertorial instead of legitimate news. The White Hat SEO interpretation is that adding one branded link back to the website of the company sending out the press release is OK, but spamming by inserting multiple exact match anchor links is not.

So with the diminished SEO value of press releases, what is the point of using them? An overlooked point is that press releases should actually be newsworthy. A new certification, office location, high profile hire, or industry award all provide good content for a press release. Press releases and newswires are read mostly by journalists, highly jaded and cynical writers who are often freelancers paid per impression on their articles. Journalists cruise newswires looking for angles that will play well in the news websites they write for. They will avoid cheap PR sites and focus on more reputable ones. Journalists will pick up company news if and only if

1. The topic is trending, and

2. It fits (or can be made to fit) their angle, and

3. The subject fits the category of news site they write for, and

4. They're afraid a competitor will publish the story first.

The practice of journalists getting paid per impression, or paid with exposure and not money, creates a huge pressure to get eyeballs on news stories. This pressure can lead to an unintended spin on content and misleading headlines, not unlike the childhood game of telephone, where players whisper a phrase around a circle, with the original message becoming quickly confused in an often hilarious way. The internet journalism machine can be summed up in two quotes from Ryan Holiday's exposé, *Trust Me, I'm Lying*: "Every decision a publisher makes is ruled by one dictum: traffic by any means" and "They aren't going to write about you, your clients, or your story unless it can be turned into a headline that will drive traffic." Holiday is the director of marketing for American Apparel and has been a media strategist for Tucker Max and other clients.[xiv]

BLACK HAT LINK BUILDING

While this book will not instruct how to do Black Hat SEO, it will provide an example of how the author's website was attacked by a Black Hat hacker for SEO purposes. SearcherMag.net, like the majority of websites using a content management system, is powered by the WordPress platform.[xv] Black Hat hackers frequently choose WordPress as the target of malicious software (called exploits) in order to have the widest reach. Through an unknown delivery method, SearcherMag.net was infected by the pharma hack, a thoroughly nasty piece of code that inserted over 100 links to vendors of male enhancement pills. Link injection is fairly common and can be easily fixed, but the pharma hack took things to another level by styling the toxic links so they're hidden from human eyes but fully visible to search engines. The addition of 100+ links to Russian pharmacies had an immediate negative effect on organic search rankings. After the links were discovered in a monthly sweep, SearcherMag.net quickly purged them, only to have them resurrect a month later! As it turned out, the pharma hack embeds itself in core code and the WordPress database, with complete removal coming only by wiping and reinstalling the entire website.

Cui bono—who benefits? The pharma hack isn't the work of some script kiddie fooling around—it's a meticulously engineered Black Hat SEO effort to build millions of links. The genius of it is that the links get mass-placed on a highly diverse variety of legitimate, Google-friendly websites which then boost the linked pages in search results. Thousands of people search Google daily for the term "buy cialis without prescription." Black Hat SEO consultants point all these links to a variety of disposable, interlinked websites and then route the generated traffic directly to offshore pharmacies. Pharma products, whether fake or genuine, are expensive and have enormous profit margins. Selling pharma product links makes for a get-rich-quick scenario of sorts, with the top male enhancement terms estimated to bring over $100,000 in revenue per day. In the lead-generation arena, the keyword of choice for Black Hat SEO is "payday loan," with similar earning potential. Of course, Google's engineers will eventually find and account for such manipulation of search results, but this can take weeks or months to iron out.

SEO: CONTENT IS KING

Creating mediocre content is easy. Creating awesome content that people will happily share is hard work, and is increasingly in forms other than the written word. Later this chapter discusses strategies with images and interactive media that are highly effective when combined with a healthy blogging system.

BLOGGING IS EXCELLENT SEO

Blogging and guest articles are a fantastic way for brands both large and small to generate links that boost SEO. Unfortunately, it's completely ineffective if not done right. There are two main mistakes made in blogging: inconsistent blogging, or **not blogging at all**.

Even Fortune 500 companies make the mistake of not blogging. It is difficult, especially in highly technical or deep niches, to find writers who can produce great content, not to mention finding topics of interest to the target audience, if not viral. But it must happen. The top-of-funnel audience is looking for information and industry news. If, when these people visit a website, a blog page is either not present or updated infrequently, mindshare is lost. However, the true opportunity cost is the lost ability to have great content spread and expand the top of the lead-generation funnel wide across the internet.

What's worse than no content? **Crappy content.** Avoid writing content that is

- **"Stuffed"**—Companies should resist the urge to plug their brand every third word. Readers and other bloggers enjoy original, objective, and useful content, not marketing copy.

- **Plagiarized**—In the new age of authorship, it's easier to determine plagiarism than ever before. Google can detect it automatically if the original article uses the G+ Author tag, and ranks accordingly.

- **Repackaged**—Covering industry news is a good move, but add company personality back in. Provide more value than a news article.

- **Badly Written**—For a lot of companies, finding an internal asset who can write, write well, and has time to write is effectively impossible. If it's not a fit, don't settle for less.

- **Isolated**—For blogging to work, it must reach an audience far beyond the website. Use email subscriptions, social media, and third parties to push.

Blogging can take months or years to build an audience that actually leaves comments and interacts. Companies should be careful not to expect instantaneous results.

ARTICLE MARKETING

The ultimate one-way broadcast, article submissions were for many years the king of SEO techniques. Generating lots of low-quality content articles then spraying them out to hundreds or thousands of article directories was a low-cost, high-impact, and largely automated way to gain valuable backlinks. However, Google reacted in an innovative way: by applying quality penalties directly to the article directories. By lowering the authority of these article farms, the links out from these sites were massively devalued as well. When the algorithm changed, many business owners, surprised to learn that their SEO rankings were derived from this practice, watched their search engine traffic drop drastically.

Avoiding article marketing penalties is simple with these guidelines:

- Provide good content. Articles should be held to near the same standard as blog content: objective, original, unique.

- Solve a problem. Unlike blog posts which are typically informational in nature, an article should answer a question or provide some tangible value to a reader.

- Consider the source. Just a handful of article directories, like Squidoo.com and Wikihow, are still authoritative in the eyes of search engines. Avoid poorly regarded directories with broad topics; if anybody can provide articles, the directory probably won't provide much value and may even carry a penalty.

- Promote the articles. Articles without any social or external references don't have much value.

Keeping these points in mind, article marketing is still an effective way to build links. However, companies that have run SEO campaigns through the years should audit existing links to ensure that the linking sites are high-quality. Just a few low-quality linking websites can ruin an entire backlink portfolio by causing ranking penalties that are difficult to remove.

VIDEO: UNBELIEVABLY EFFECTIVE SEO

To learn that video SEO is effective, we need go no farther than the first result in many Google searches. The only thing worse than no internet video strategy is bad internet video strategy. But why do so many companies fail to create compelling video marketing, or fail to even try? The short answer is that high-quality video is difficult and expensive to produce. It must have the right ingredients: a relevant concept, a well-written script, talented actors, an experienced video crew, an appropriate location or green screen, good lighting, clear audio, high production values, a competent editor, and perhaps most importantly, a realistic budget. For video presented in a professional setting like a YouTube ad or on a landing page, all elements must be present. Due to audio and visual quality limitations, videos shot with a smartphone or webcam aren't appropriate for professional selling, even when highly edited. Editing is a highly technical process typically requiring expensive software and someone skilled in transitions, color correction, and sound engineering.

Even with a professional camera crew and editor, it's still possible to produce a dud. In video, storytelling is everything, and without a compelling message and presentation, visitors lose interest in seconds.

After the lengthy process of marrying a good story to talented people then shooting and producing high-quality high video content, marketing begins. The video has to be distributed; simply posting on YouTube or the company blog won't take it viral. But how to promote video?

- AdWords for Video (YouTube) is a great way to get exposure; advertisers pay for each viewing

- In-stream video ads with a network like BrightRoll.com (large cash commitment)

- Traditional television advertising (largest cash commitment)

- SEO—linking to and building citations and mentions around the video

- Internal promotion—announcements on email subscriber lists or websites or landing pages

SEO FOR GRAPHICS AND INTERACTIVES

Infographics, a popular form of content, deliver value through visually representing data in a way that is easily understood. As with any other content, it must speak to an audience, be of excellent quality, and have high production values. Unfortunately, since infographics are typically a large image file in

PNG or JPEG format, they do nothing for SEO as is. Follow these best practices when creating infographics[xvi]:

- Create an infographic landing page with a text version of infographic content.

- Research keywords beforehand and associate these keywords with the infographic.

- Make sure metadata like Open Graph and Page Title are set and include keywords.

THE ROLE OF FLASH IN SEO

Flash is no longer the interactive media of choice. Once highly popular as a trendy website design method, this format found a strong enemy in no less than Steve Jobs, who essentially made it his sole mission to destroy the format, namely through disabling it on all Apple iPhones.[xvii] Furthermore, the compiling of text and pages into a single Flash file proved difficult for Google to read and index, and eventually brought about ranking penalties for websites created with this method.

FLASH IN INTERNET ADVERTISING

If there is anything redeeming about Flash as a technology, it's that it makes designing and publishing content relatively simple. Although Flash has little role in online marketing, it lives on in banner advertising, where it can be a quick and cost-effective way to bring motion and interaction to a static image ad. In fact, many third-party ad networks encourage the use of Flash ads due to small file sizes and consistent experience. But even this use is being overtaken by HTML5; big players like Google Display Network prefer the new format, with pressure coming from the ever-growing mobile audience.

WHEN SOCIAL MARKETING CAN GENERATE LEADS

Social media marketing is a necessary evil in the modern lead-generation campaign. Look no farther than the exponential growth into public offerings of Twitter (over 225 million users) and Facebook (1.1 billion users), as well as the somewhat disputed[xviii] 300 million reported users of dark horse Google+. Traditional marketing promotion has been turned upside down by the rise of social networking, and new strategies are needed to adapt to the changing conditions. As a recent article notes, "However, it is no longer enough to merely incorporate social media as standalone elements of a marketing plan. Companies need to consider both social *and* traditional media as part of an ecosystem whereby all elements work together toward a common objective."[xix]

BUT WHAT IF MY BRAND GOES VIRAL?

Of the 12 million websites launched per year,[xx] only a couple go viral. When this happens, the legendary four-hour workweek on the tropical island can finally be achieved. But why is viral an unrealistic goal?

- Viral is an unpredictable, organic, behaviorally driven process that is difficult to reverse engineer. A 2014 analysis of over 7,000 *Wall Street Journal* articles showed that viral content must play to high-arousal emotions of the right audience, and be shared by the right high-status people.[xxi]

- Attempts at this type of campaign often ignore that viral campaigns require remarkable products and brilliant concepts, and even multimillion-dollar budgets fail to guarantee success.

- The viral campaign has to be uniquely funny, creative, or "cool," and behind the scenes this is actually a ton of work to manufacture. Dollar Shave Club hired a Los Angeles–based ad agency to shoot their viral YouTube video, which was heavily planned, scripted, and edited as well as directed by comedian Lucia Aniello.[xxii]

- Viral intent can often backfire. A recent Toyota Matrix campaign where the audience members were encouraged to have a fictional persona stalk their friends was settled in a $10 million lawsuit.[xxiii]

Story short, even with a ton of money and time invested, the odds are strongly against going viral by accident. With about twenty hours of new footage getting added to YouTube per minute, business owners have a better chance of winning the lottery.[xxiv]

THERE IS NO SILVER BULLET

Social media is a highly diverse yet interconnected ecosystem. A one-size-fits-all approach fails because the reality is that the social media solution for each company is unique. To build or expand a social media audience, businesses have only three real options:

1. Focus within. Zappos.com built 400,000 Facebook "likes" using nothing but a few friendly employees and an integrated set of

tools on their website enabling customers to easily share purchases on social media.[xxv]

2. Hire a consultant to help create a social strategy. But beware of specialist social media experts. Often not well-rounded, those who claim to exclusively work with social media ignore other pieces of the puzzle like sales methodology, customer service, and branding.

3. Hire an agency that includes social media consulting as part of its offering. This type of agency falls into two categories: the first is a full-service agency that does everything, and the second is typically a niche player that will provide PR, content development, SEO, and other closely related services.

Regardless of the approach, an effective social media marketing campaign often contains advertising. On Facebook, the EdgeRank algorithm limits the number of fans that see an organic post. So promotion is necessary to effectively reach even an audience that has been built organically.

CAN SOCIAL BE IGNORED?

What happens to campaigns that don't have social media as an element? The truth is that not everyone needs social media. In some industries social media fails to provide an effective lead-generation ROI: financial services, consulting, and B2B, to name a few. Why is it so painful for these companies to generate leads on social media? The answer lies in user psychology. Typically, a user of social media is in a passive interaction mindset. They are consuming the updates of their friends and associates. It's a huge leap of faith to go outside the comfort of Facebook or Twitter and submit information to an external website. This is true even if this same user will share, interact with, or "like" branded content; the social platform that it occurs on has a gravity that must be overcome.

One time when companies absolutely must invest in social media is damage control. In a situation where customers or clients are airing negative reviews on sites like Yelp or having negative conversations about the product or service on Facebook, an immediate and objective response is necessary. It's basic human nature to warn friends about danger, and that is why negative reviews often go viral, even if the person posting them doesn't have a large audience. Only one influencer needs to see and respond for the negativity to spread. The case of Ocean Marketing and "wwwebsite on the internet" is one such story, where a rude email exchange forwarded to a journalist prompted the public shaming, industry disavowal, and immediate firing of the PR firm in question.[xxvi] Savvy brands beware lest negative content be the type that goes viral.

DOING SOCIAL RIGHT

The name of the social game is legitimacy, which only happens at massive scale. The author joined LinkedIn in 2008 but didn't get a first referral until 2012, after acquiring about 400 connections. There are profiles on LinkedIn with thousands or hundreds of thousands of connections. Guy Kawasaki, a LinkedIn celebrity, has over 400,000 followers. The perception of legitimacy by numbers extends to Facebook, where a brand needs at least 1,000 Facebook fans, and Twitter, where about 10,000 followers are needed to avoid being perceived as "second class."

Unfortunately, doing social right requires labor-intensive maintenance. Larger businesses are forced to hire a social media manager who can monitor 24/7 for both positive and negative interactions.

Automated interaction is quickly recognized and discarded by the people who can become a company's best fans. A lack of human interaction creates connections or fans that have no real value. Ignoring people by not responding or reciprocating to messages and retweets is an effective way to communicate that a company does not care about its fans. If a business is too small to hire a dedicated employee to manage social media, the owner typically gets stuck with the responsibility. When outsourcing this type of work, be prepared to pay top dollar for someone with good communication skills and business knowledge who can represent the company in a high-quality way. Offshore or bottom-dollar firms just aren't worth the risk to a company's reputation.

RESPECT MY AUTHORITY

For businesses seeking to establish expertise in their niche, there are some additional options beyond the chatter of Facebook, Twitter, and Google+. Question-and-answer sites—also known as authority websites—like Quora, Subreddits, Yahoo Answers, and LinkedIn Groups can be an effective way to prospect, but all too often these sites just provide a digital way to argue with other industry insiders. The authority play works best with a broad niche; if what the company does is very specific, there's typically not much of a community. When joining an active authority discussion, expect some meddling from the resident experts, which may vary from negativity to in some cases outright abuse.

Unlike other social media that operate with the frenzy of "right now," authority sites move at a snail's pace. Opinions that aren't carefully informed, objective, and backed up with multiple citations will be ignored or mocked. While spelling and grammar errors are forgiven or encouraged in tweets (posts on Twitter), less than perfect English on an authority website can be used as an easy rebuttal to just about any point made. However the conversation takes place, the only thing that's certain is that the discussion thread will be around forever. Popular threads can appear for years in search results on the social media site, and in some cases even in Google searches, according to platform and privacy settings.

FORUMS STILL WORK

Older than the internet, forums are an underutilized and often overlooked part of the social strategy. Forums work best for specific niches or narrow audiences; a quick Google search for [keyword] + forum will turn up at least a couple of forum websites targeted directly at the topic. As a whole, the internet is trending away from this type of interaction and audiences are declining over time, but a healthy if somewhat eccentric community still exists in just about any imaginable subcategory. If SEO is a factor in deciding whether to invest time in forums, be careful to select forums with public posts. If all content is locked behind a login and invisible to search engines, there's little point in building links.

Members of forums and authority sites can be cool to newcomers. Forum communities have distinct personalities and can be rather fascist in enforcing community rules. For example, most forums will ban users who are excessively self-promotional, and some ban new users who post too many new threads.

No internet community is complete without a few trolls and at least one overzealous moderator. The trolls usually work by posting hateful comments or starting arguments, and they thrive on negative reactions. The moderators are unpaid volunteers— a business model that has proved quite lucrative for the massive forum site Reddit (valued in 2012 at $240 million[xxvii])—who spend a large part of their free time policing their area of the forum. To avoid the moderators, trolls commonly register ten or more fake accounts and may conduct entirely fake conversations.

In between this drama, there are some real conversations that have value. It's possible to get to know the active posters in the forum and make valuable networking or business connections. Though the leads generated in forums are typically few and far between, they are usually made up with in quality.

PUSHING LEADS WITH ONLINE ADVERTISING

When running internet advertising, there are quite a few choices of channels, and networks within those channels. This chapter will cover everything from search and display ads, to email and affiliate programs, as well as the pros and cons of each.

SEARCH ADVERTISING

Search advertising, also known as PPC or SEM, is an arena dominated by Google AdWords, which has over 70% of the market. Second, and still of noteworthy mention, is Microsoft Bing. Since Microsoft's acquisition of Yahoo Search in 2010, Bing has become the second largest player, with approximately 25% of the market. Following its recent technological improvements, Bing's search engine is remarkably similar to Google's, albeit lacking the social integration and fine-tuned performance attributes of AdWords. Nonetheless, it remains a strong competitor and is appropriate for some campaigns.

What's left? Rounding out the bottom 5% of search market share is an long list of networks. These include BidVertiser, 7Search, Trafficvance, Ask.com, AltaVista, and many other names that rarely meet the public eye. This tier of search traffic usually has a lower ROI than Google and Bing, as well as a far smaller audience. Running campaigns on these bottom-tier networks is suggested only if a company can first maximize ad spends in existing Google and Yahoo search campaigns. However, certain niche products or services can find the specialized audiences of these bottom-tier networks very attractive.

SOCIAL ADVERTISING

The 800-pound gorilla in this space is Facebook. Facebook is technically social advertising, although it works more like display advertising. (More on that in the next section.) Facebook is a CPM (cost per thousand) platform, where advertisers pay for impressions (eyeballs), not clicks as with CPC (cost per click). All that personal data users put in their Facebook profiles is sold to advertisers to target ads. Facebook seems, though, to have at times an adversarial role with media buyers. For example, only in January 2013 did Facebook release a publically supported conversion code.[xxviii] (Lead-generation advertisers require conversion code to calculate CPA and other vital conversion statistics.) There is no better way to communicate "We don't care about your conversion rate" than to go for years without offering a conversion code. Some speculate that Facebook wanted to discourage the use of external landing pages, instead forcing advertisers to use destination pages hosted on Facebook to increase their brand equity. Either way, it's clear that Facebook leans more towards brand-type advertising than direct response. Lead-generation campaigns there do work, but they are tricky.

Let's say a company did the responsible thing and organically cultivated a huge fan base around its brand. Welcome to EdgeRank, Facebook's algorithm that limits post visibility to just 16% of a page's audience. Of course, promoting the post to more eyeballs is possible for an additional fee. When investing time in Facebook, just remember that it's the platform where a company can build an audience then have to pay to access them.

Facebook does excel in certain industries like politics and social causes, and with products like shoes, video, and food. It is not a first-choice vehicle for lead generation.

Effective social ad campaigns are usually surrounded with promotional and marketing campaigns. Rarely direct response and rarely sold on a cost-per-click basis, social ads on Facebook, Twitter, Instagram, and similar sites are very unlike the other ad channels mentioned in this chapter.

B2B SOCIAL ADS WITH LINKEDIN

A notable exception for the lead-generation space is LinkedIn, which boasts a $63 million per quarter ad business.[xxix] For B2B companies, there is no more targeted way to reach their audience. All the information users put in their profile, such as job title, company, and education, is fully targetable, allowing some very precise campaigns. LinkedIn seems to be constantly innovating, allowing companies to run CPC ads and include a lead capture feature—allowing advertisers to capture the LinkedIn contact info leads without leaving LinkedIn. Short, sweet, and highly targeted ads seem to work best. For salespeople on a budget, the popular InMail tool (allowing advertisers to pay to message contacts outside their sphere of influence) is highly effective, with response guaranteed.[xxx] It's also possible to Black Hat spam LinkedIn contacts with mass messaging software, though the community frowns on this.

DISPLAY ADVERTISING

Banners are the granddaddy of internet advertising. In the early '90s, banner ads were manually placed by webmasters, quickly giving way to small niche advertising networks. Through a series of mergers and acquisitions, most of these networks consolidated under the control of Google, using the trade names Google Display Network and DoubleClick. Although other display ad networks like Yahoo! Bing Network Contextual Ads, Adblade, Advertising.com, AppNexus and Chikita exist, none have quite the reach of Google.

The quality of the ad varies with the platform. Google has some fairly stringent guidelines on what sort of ads it will allow on its platform. The obnoxious screaming WIN A FREE APPLE IPOD NANO ad is limited to lower-tier networks.

Display ads are almost exclusively sold on a CPM basis. While networks will calculate CPC as a courtesy, display is all about eyeballs. However, if targeted correctly, display ads can be a valuable asset to any lead-generation campaign. Most display targeting is contextual, based on either the website where the ads appear or the words surrounding the ad.

DISPLAY REMARKETING

Everyone who has abandoned an online purchase has seen the annoying purchase-related ad that keeps showing up afterward. This is behavioral targeting AKA remarketing or retargeting. Savvy advertisers use remarketing to add a layer of targeting to an otherwise broad banner ad campaign. From a lead-generation perspective, remarketing can generate some of the hottest and also most cost-effective leads possible. Although the audience is typically very limited—with the exception of popular, high traffic sites—the cookie-based targeting makes for a very engaging and motivating ad.

NATIVE ADVERTISING

Native advertising is "a form of paid media where the ad experience follows the natural form and function of the user experience in which it is placed."[xxxi]

In other words, the site designs the ads. The goal of any native advertisement is to insert the sponsored message into the content in such a way that it feels natural and welcoming to the visitor. An extremely difficult trick to pull off consistently, native advertising remains the bane of news websites and publishers trying to monetize their content. Since native advertising varies on a per-placement basis, it is never available to traditional ad networks like the Google Display Network (GDN) and has to be individually negotiated with the publishing website. The beautiful thing about native advertising is that nobody can agree on what it actually *is*. Vooza.com, a 2013 native-advertising startup, produces sarcastic and hilarious videos about startup culture. Into these messages they blend paid advertiser messages, allowing access to the Vooza audience. The main key of native advertising is that it be a seamless and enhanced experience for the end user. As in any ad campaign, audience and message must be tightly related, but native advertising sets the bar even higher. Proponents of this technique argue that traditional banner and popup advertising is an intrusive and annoying experience to the user. Arguments against it voice concerns that the integrity of brands can get compromised if a clear line is not drawn between paid message and actual content. Native advertising is a relatively new field and is constantly evolving.

CPV

A lot of free software today is monetized through the use of popunder CPV (cost per view) traffic. This type of traffic uses the CPM model, where a company pays for impressions and not click-throughs. The ad networks that specialize in this space distribute toolbars, emoticons, and other dubious free software that installs adware on the host computer. Personal financial information is not at risk, but programs of this type can cause home-page hijacking, the appearance of unexpected links, or a slowdown in computer function. The audience for adware tends to be an older demographic that is not fully computer literate or is otherwise unable or unmotivated to remove the infection. Advertisers that are successful with CPV campaigns tend be in gray areas such as remote PC help, male enhancement pills, diet supplements, multilevel marketing, and similar ventures.

ACQUISITION EMAIL VS NEWSLETTERS

Email traffic is sold either on a CPC or CPS (cost per sent email) basis. Email advertising is strictly unsolicited bulk email (known in the industry as *acquisition email*), as opposed to permission-based newsletter marketing with providers like

MailChimp and Constant Contact. Bulk email is blasted out to huge email lists that are rented or harvested with a direct-response message. Due to the complex systems that relay mail across the internet and the actions of spam watchdog groups like the Spamhaus Project, it's common for just 30% of spam sent to be delivered, and of that, fewer than 10% of the recipients will open the email, and of that typically 2 to 3% will click the link to the landing page. A mailer (industry term for bulk emailer) needs to get out a lot of email to make any money, and thus some of the higher end systems can pump out one million sends *per hour*. But as quickly as mailers deploy higher volume systems, the servers on the receiving end fight back with ever more sophisticated spam blacklisting and digital fingerprinting technology. This arms race makes it impossible for amateurs to play at the game; it's estimated that 95% of the world's spam is generated by fifteen or fewer individuals.

While spam is annoying, contrary to popular belief, sending it is completely legal, provided that the message includes opt-out instructions and complies with the few basic provisions in the CAN-SPAM act.[xxxii] The penalties for failing to observe CAN-SPAM are massive, including fines and injunctions by the Federal Trade Commission. Regrettably for advertisers, government entities may come knocking even if it was an affiliate or network that violated the law while promoting an offer. Risk aside, there are hundreds of millions of active email addresses out there, and certain types of people will make decisions based on junk email. With the ultradirect response focus of an email, the medium is ideal for brands both with name recognition and those without. Email is a key piece of a successful lead-generation strategy, especially for financial industry products like mortgage, tax relief, debt settlement, and related services.

AFFILIATE PROGRAMS

Affiliate programs are referral programs in which a business has no direct contact with the people who generate leads; instead, an offer is placed via an affiliate network, and a commission is paid each time a lead is generated. To advertisers who have an in-demand service, affiliate programs provide massive scale in exchange for limited control over message and placement. The parties who generate the leads are called publishers; the ad network is simply a marketplace that connects them with advertiser offers. Publishers use a variety of media to drive leads, all of which are covered in this book. The advertiser does have the ability to limit the media channels, as well as the creatives (email content such as message body, subject lines, and sender address) used by publishers that promote their offer, although this is sometimes loosely enforced by the network.

The bad aspects of affiliate marketing AKA performance marketing are

- The advertiser loses control of the message.

- There are limited opportunities to participate. Networks screen advertisers religiously and seek only one or two offers in each industry.

- It's an extremely incestuous business. Offers are often resold or white-labeled multiple times across different networks, making it even more difficult to identify or regulate traffic sources.

- Promotion often is by gray-area traffic like email and CPV.

- Advertiser competition is fierce, with many similar offerings.

- Fraud and fake leads are common.

Businesses that have a competitive service, a fair price with room for affiliate commissions, and a solid handle on their sales funnel should sign up with an affiliate network. There are several versions of do-it-yourself affiliate program software that cut out the network, and this can be a viable option, assuming a company has the time and resources to run it properly. In this case, the major challenge will be recruiting and retaining affiliates, something the network usually handles. Affiliates, especially the few that can drive lead volume, are wary of advertisers and can rarely be located, let alone approached to run offers.

ADS THAT HIT
THE BULL'S-EYE

One of the greatest advantages to online advertising versus traditional advertising is precise and specific targeting. Online, there is a treasure trove of data available about any given person, including the website where the advertisement is displayed; the user's IP address, cookies, and device; and even behavioral data from logged-in users. This section attempts to list all the methods of targeting available in a general sense. Many ad networks or media have unique targeting options, with methods and results varying widely.

GEOTARGETING

The ability to target an internet ad based on user location is surprising to most nontechnical people. This capability results from a basic component of internet technology, the IP address. This numerical range can be traced with a high degree of certainty back to the city where the computer is located. A common question is "How does geotargeting work on a mobile phone?" It depends which media is serving the ad. Android phones report their precise GPS coordinators to Google's servers, making it more accurate to geotarget a mobile user than a desktop user.

Where It Went Right

Advertiser Type: City councilman

Problem: Voting district is divided by zip code

Solution: Run AdWords campaign with banner ads geotargeted towards users within district zip codes

When targeting by location, it is sometimes important to distinguish between user location and intent. Google AdWords does a great job of this by allowing bids on keywords containing a location term. So if a user located in Detroit, Michigan, searches for "investment property Sacramento," the user location might not matter to a Sacramento-based realty firm.

Google excels at geotargeting mostly because they have the most user data and largest ad inventory. Although there are billions of search queries and impressions on the global scale daily, when zoomed into a zip code, there is much less inventory available. Since Google controls 70% of search market share and its publishing network GDN includes 92% of all websites, campaigns with extremely small geotargeting can still spend a sizable budget. This is strictly not the case with niche ad networks or other online advertising methods. For example, it is basically impossible to geotarget bulk email campaigns with current technology. Likewise, in today's SEO environment one must choose to promote a site locally or on the nationwide stage (and if the latter, be prepared for ultraheavy competition).

DAYPARTING

Dayparting, or limiting the days of the week or times ads can show, are used by many large advertisers to eliminate wasteful ad spends.

Dayparting is a somewhat controversial feature. While highly effective, it can have a unpredictable effect on campaign performance if not set correctly because users research on Google for days or weeks before buying some products or services. Dayparting should always follow a deep campaign analysis. A good strategy is to break down by the hour the amount and cost per conversion of a campaign. It is possible, for example, that conversions that occur between 9 pm and 4 am are much cheaper than those generated during the day.

Dayparting should be used carefully to avoid harming the search funnel. For example, though conversions are costly during the hours of 9 am to 5 pm, searchers may just be starting their research during this time and end up converting that night, or even days or weeks later. Dayparting can prevent ads from showing to these leads at a critical stage of the process. Recent modifications to Google

AdWords allow insight into "assist clicks," linking initial clicks (usually broad terms) with converting clicks that occur days, weeks, or even months later. It can be wasteful to apply dayparting without monitoring and adjusting for changes in the search funnel. Dayparting may remove a critical and unseen link between customer activity and conversion.

PLACEMENT TARGETING

An old and reliable way to target banner ads is by limiting the websites that display the ad. A large amount of demographic data is available based on the audience that visits a specific domain name. For example, an advertiser looking to reach an audience interested in a wealthier, older demographic might run ads on the domain DrudgeReport.com. (See the chart below.) Nearly every content or media site that sells advertising directly will have detailed audience information including gender, age, income, and more.

DRUDGEREPORT.COM US AUDIENCE

Source: https://www.quantcast.com/drudgereport.com?qcLocale=en_US

Some best practices when running placement-targeted ads include

- Designing advertisements that match the color, format, and style of the placements

- Ensuring message and copy are relevant to placement audience

- Tracking conversions on a domain placement level and optimizing accordingly

The Google Display Network is an advertiser-friendly network that allows a high degree of placement control with fine-tuned reporting.

DEVICE TARGETING

People use the internet on one of four types of devices: mobile, tablet, desktop, and TV. Many ad networks offer targeting down to a specific device type. Google AdWords, for example, allows the creation of separate ads for mobile devices within a campaign. Though it isn't usually possible to target specific device brands or operating systems, advertisers can target ads to users of a specific app through Google Play or iTunes.

DEMOGRAPHIC TARGETING

Instead of running ads on a website with a given audience demographic, an advertiser can run ads on a website and choose to limit ad display to a specific demographic of the site's visitors. Since the demographic data is determined by user profile, this targeting usually can't be combined with search-based advertising. Reliability is not guaranteed, as users routinely lie about age, gender, and income, especially on dating websites like OkCupid and PlentyOfFish. The targetable options vary widely, with Facebook having the most and best quality of demographic data.

CONTEXTUAL TARGETING

Instead of targeting by site, contextual targeting works by placing ads near content that is relevant to the advertiser's keywords. The network attempts to determine the topic of any given web page based on a semantic keyword analysis. Google employs a specialized version of organic spider to draw automatic instant conclusions about any website using a very sophisticated categorization system. This determination governs the amount the Google will pay AdSense publishers for clicks. Other ad networks operate in much the same way.

Where It Went Wrong

Advertiser Type: Reverse mortgage lender

Campaign: Display network ads targeting senior interest websites and blogs

Problem: Traffic and ad spend spiked

Analysis: Manual examination revealed several placements were fake websites that fraudulently sent traffic; Google credited ad spend

KEYWORD TARGETING

Google created search advertising in 1999 by allowing advertisers to bid on keywords searched by users, a program known as AdWords. It remains one of the most effective direct response advertising online today. With 5.9 billion searches on Google per day[xxxiii] (about 2.7 billion on Bing) it's imperative to set keywords properly. AdWords offers five different types of keywords: broad, phrase, exact, modifier, and negative. Best practices include precise setting and optimizing of all match types.

Where It Went Wrong

Advertiser Type: Mortgage company

Campaign: Ran display network advertisements targeted at the "harp" keyword, intending to capture traffic interest in the Home Affordable Refinance Program (HARP)

Problem: Advertisements ran on searches like "harp music lessons" and "harpsichords"

Analysis: Contextual keyword too broad

RETARGETING: SELF-AWARE BANNER ADS

"In the 21st century, the database is the marketplace."

—Stan Rapp, MRM Partners Worldwide

Retargeting, in a nutshell, is the process of delivering an ad to a user based on that user's prior online activity. Retargeting (also known as remarketing) is a simple concept: advertisements are more relevant if they are tailored to a user's current behavior. The specific action a user took today or recently is often far more relevant than other more available targeting such as age or search history. Truly impressive is how accessible user information like page views, search history, and offline data is to advertisers. Unfortunately in today's online advertising world, the retargeting space is highly fragmented with many competing and overlapping providers, making it difficult to plan and launch this type of campaign.

HOW IT WORKS, CLIENT SIDE

The foundation of retargeting is the lowly browser cookie.[xxxiv] Also known as an HTTP cookie or web cookie, this small text file is set by a website and stored on the user's computer. First introduced by Netscape in 1994, cookies are an integrated part of the internet. They perform many useful functions such as authentication, which allows users to stay logged in to sites like Facebook. Cookies also serve an important role in website visitor tracking, which powers everything from Google Analytics to affiliate marketing networks to live chat scripts. In the context of retargeting, cookies allow the tracking of a given user's browsing or search history. This history is stored, not in the cookie itself, but in a centralized database online. Cookies are typically just a reference to this database, which is owned by an ad network or data aggregator.

HOW IT WORKS, NETWORK SIDE

Ad networks provide publisher sites (content sites such as ESPN.com) with ad server code. This code, placed on the pages that site visitors see, determines in real time which ad to display. The simplest use of ad server technology is to execute a media buy for site placement targeting, as discussed in Chapter 11. In retargeting, the code sends the visitor's IP address and cookie data to the ad server. If this data matches a retargeting media buy, then that ad will be sent instead. Retargeting is great for publishers because advertisers are often willing to pay much more for retargeting than for placement, resulting in higher CPM and higher earnings for the publisher. A 1:1 relationship between advertiser and ad network is the simplest use of retargeting, but often is much more involved.

ROLE OF AD NETWORKS

The Google Display Network is the largest display ad network, covering approximately 60% of the internet. Retargeting, a standard feature inside AdWords, is a simple and easy way to deploy this type of campaign. Over twenty major ad networks cover the remaining 40%, including Facebook Exchange (FBX). Certain providers such as AdRoll act as an intermediary to these networks, allowing advertisers to get the widest possible reach. In order for a retargeting ad to actually reach a given person, this person must be online and browsing a website that is "in network."

GETTING COOKIES: CLICKSTREAM DATA

The most common way to build retargeting cookie lists is placing a pixel-sized image on all pages of the advertiser's website. In a common lead-generation scenario, traffic is sent to a page to fill out a form. Building a good remarketing list for lead generation is as simple as gathering data about the visitors who viewed the key page but didn't view the thank-you page. This filtered list contains data about visitors who clicked on an ad or otherwise showed interest in an offer but didn't convert into a lead, and targeting ads to them is a high-ROI "second bite of the apple." Filtering the conversion page is a best practice to minimize wasted ad spends. In this scenario, common to GDN and AdRoll campaigns, the generated list is considered to be owned by the advertiser (though it is stored anonymously on the provider's server). Google Analytics can also generate retargeting lists, although it is specific to the Google Display Network only.

OFFLINE DATA ONBOARDING AND FIRST-PARTY DATA

As described above, the retargeting system serves hyper-relevant ads based on cookie data. For advertisers who don't have much web traffic or big databases, there is another option. Through a data onboarding service, it's possible to take stored customer or prospect data, and cookie match. For example, an advertiser with customer relationship management software, such as Salesforce, can export aged leads and serve retargeting ads to them. In addition, advertisers operating call centers or sending direct mail campaigns have additional data retargeting opportunities. This new and highly sophisticated technique helps advertisers get better ROI on all their other lead-generation efforts. With data onboarding, it's usually possible to match about 40% to 60% of any given data to actual cookies that can be added to a retargeting list. What's truly surprising is how little data is needed to make the match: some vendors can cookie-match based solely on missed calls to a call center. The only limit is the original first-party database; campaigns of this type require a minimum of 50,000 unique records, aged within 30 to 120 days.

THIRD-PARTY DATA AND MODELING

At the bottom of the retargeting rabbit hole is Big Data. Data management platforms (DMPs) are an audience data marketplace. An advertiser looking to get maximum return on its clickstream and first-party data will upload it to a DMP. The DMP will then model the data to get a scientific understanding of it, then expand the retargeting list *to include similar user cookies*. Incredibly, a DMP can expand the size of a given retargeting list by a 6:1 or more ratio. Until recently, data modeling was off-limits to everyone but the largest and most sophisticated advertisers, but new techniques and vendors entering the industry are making data modeling more and more accessible.

MESSAGING AND SEGMENTATION

The best retargeting messaging is simple and direct. Since the leads are in the Decision part of the funnel, they need a clear nudge to purchase. Messaging that includes a discount or added value is always a good idea. A well-written retargeting ad reminds the user of the brand and concept, and pushes them back towards conversion. It's important to exclude converted visitors from the retargeting list, and it's also important to segment the leads to be retargeted. For advertisers with long or complex sales cycles, segmentation can be an especially powerful tool. Some great areas of segmentation are length of time on page, key page, status of lead, interaction with a newsletter, and download of a case study. The more specific and behavior-based the ad message can be, the more effective the campaign.

PRIVACY AND LEGAL MATTERS

Retargeting by nature is highly personal and somewhat controversial. Several pieces of "Do Not Track" legislation have been introduced, starting with the "Do Not Track Me Online Act of 2011," which governs the collection and use of personal information.[xxxv] This bill and others like it require that any use or sharing of personal information should be disclosed in a website's privacy policy. Ad networks can still offer retargeting with impunity because the data is aggregated and specific users are not identified. As of this writing, there is still no global opt-out list that would allow consumers to prevent themselves from being tracked for retargeting and other purposes. Advocacy groups such as Consumer Watchdog and Consumers Union are pushing for such legislation, stating that the online equivalent of "Do Not Call" is necessary, especially to protect the privacy of teens under eighteen years of age.[xxxvi]

Savvy consumers simply install a browser-based tool like AdBlock Pro, which finds and deletes ad server codes from websites in real time, providing an advertisement-free internet. For the ultra-privacy-minded, there are tools like NoScript, which completely remove all JavaScript. There's always the option of simply turning cookies off; but without cookies or JavaScript, most websites on the internet are unusable. Many people have simply accepted retargeting as a fact of online life, and even prefer behavior-targeted ads over those that are blindly and irrelevantly targeted. Instead of using Google, one can experience truly anonymous search through the portal DuckDuckGo.com, which is funded by the Don't Track Us initiative.[xxxvii]

ROI-BASED ANALYTICS

One of the major benefits of online lead generation is that it's much more measurable and auditable than offline advertising. Internet technology allows amazing insights into the performance of online ad spends. Key performance indicators are impressions, clicks, conversions, and cost.

IMPRESSIONS

An impression is defined as a single time an advertisement is displayed to a user. Traffic bought on a CPM basis, like ads on the Google Display

Network, will be billed based on the number of impressions accrued. In email marketing, the number of emails that are opened counts as impressions. In affiliate marketing, the number of impressions is rarely reported to the advertiser, with clicks being the primary metric.

CLICKS

The dominant means of billing advertisers for an ad spend, clicks represent a single time a user clicks on an advertisement. To the dismay of many advertisers, clicks do not always equate to leads, and all clicks aren't created equal. In certain media, click fraud runs rampant. To combat this problem, most ad networks have some sort of click tracking or uniqueness requirement in place. For example, clicks in Google AdWords are accredited by the Interactive Media Council and are periodically audited for accuracy. Google has something of a reputation in this sector, with multiple patents in click fraud detection technology. At the dawn of internet advertising, it may have been possible for companies to click on a competitor's ad until the budget was gone, but sophisticated monitoring makes this unlikely. Since keeping advertisers is cheaper than finding new ones, the incentive for the ad network to guarantee legitimate clicks is quite large.[xxxviii]

CLICK-THROUGH RATE

Click-through rate is the best leading indicator for determining the success of the creative and targeting for a given ad. (The creative is the ad's text and artwork.) Though relative, CTR demonstrates how likely the audience of an ad is to express interest by clicking. Google AdWords penalizes advertisers with low CTR rates, and other networks may red-flag such campaigns. CPM networks have little incentive to care about clicks, which is both a blessing and a curse.

CONVERSIONS

No matter what kind of advertising is being run, tracking conversions is an absolute must. Online advertising is basically useless without being able to associate actions with a dollar amount. AdWords, Facebook, Bing, and most other major ad networks offer conversion-tracking codes. A common question is "Can I trust that the conversions are accurate?" The answer in most cases is absolutely yes; the technology is quite mature, and the process is fully automated. For example, Google AdWords tracking code will not fire unless it has been placed by clicking on an AdWords ad, so conversions tracked are a very reliable indicator, unless the code has been placed on the wrong page. There are only a few scenarios where tracking isn't possible, and these are limited to users who have JavaScript or cookies disabled. The internet is essentially unusable without cookies, so this situation is limited to hardcore privacy nuts, or users with legacy devices such as old cell phones.

Affiliate networks and some ad networks use a tracking link plus pixel system. In link tracking, when the user clicks on a link it sets a cookie on the user's device. Then when the visitor submits their information as a lead and is redirected to the thank-you or confirmation page, a pixel is fired: an invisible one-pixel image in the browser references the cookie, triggering a conversion in the tracking system.

Best practice: If conversion codes are provided by the ad network, install them. If the ad network doesn't provide conversion tracking, it's also possible to configure Google Analytics or other web stats program to track lead conversions.

OPTIMIZING FOR CONVERSIONS

Google AdWords allows ad buyers to optimize on

the keyword level for conversions, making it easy to decide which keywords to delete and which keyword bids to increase. It's equally easy to identify problems with ad groups, campaigns, or any other targeting or placement. Conversion optimization is a quick and easy way to see what is working and what is not. Management of any campaign becomes much simpler and more precise.

CONVERSION AS TARGETING

When building remarketing lists, always exclude cookies from users who have already become a lead. Spending ad dollars chasing people who have already converted is a sure-fire way to annoy them and waste ad spend. In some cases, it might be good to advertise to such users, but with a separate message for a complimentary offer, or a call to action that pulls them deeper into the sales funnel, such as scheduling an appointment. Advertising to people who have already converted is called post-conversion marketing. It can be quite powerful for businesses with long sales cycles, and can be combined with other lead nurturing techniques.

TRAFFIC ANALYTICS

When traffic isn't converting well, it's time to look at the engagement that the user has on-page. Google Analytics can answer what happens after they click on the ad but before a lead conversion. Though there are many web analytics programs, Google Analytics is free, automatically integrates with AdWords and most paid media, and also works to measure SEO and social traffic sources. No matter the brand, all analytics software reports KPIs such as bounce rate, time on site, pages per visit, the user's operating system and device, which pages they visited, which page they exited from, and many other pieces of useful information.

Use Case

Problem: Low conversion

Metric: Bounce rate

Analysis: Segment traffic sources by browser type; discover that mobile users have low conversion rate

Solution: Improve user experience in mobile devices by implementing responsive design

CONCLUSION

The aim of this book is to provide the big picture of internet lead generation, from buying traffic to generating leads; to set the record straight about advertising and marketing techniques; and to explain how to drive targeted visitors that ultimately convert into leads.

"Leads are a metric that, as marketers, we have to rely on. Because leads mean money."

—Kipp Bodnar, *Inbound Marketing Strategist (B2B Marketing) at HubSpot*

AIDA is the foundation of modern marketing. Corporate websites built primarily to brand the company may fail to gather attention or interest, yet both websites and direct response advertising have become increasingly important as consumers move online and away from TV, print, radio, and direct mail. Reinvesting traditional media spending into SEM campaigns will deliver cost-effective, ultratargeted leads to the sales forces who can no longer rely on the traditional methods.

Successful SEO, content marketing, and social campaigns should be run according to best practices and the impact they have on lead generation. A fine line divides social marketing and social advertising. Leads can be generated with search ads incorporating the wide array of targeting available for any internet ads. Retargeting using the lead-generation power of the database allows the capture of lost sales. Online lead generation can and should be measured; what is the point of buying traffic if the results can't be evaluated?

Companies don't have to rely on referrals, resellers, or lead brokers to generate new sales and customers. Not only is internal lead generation profitable and scalable, but the competition is only getting fiercer. Creating a well-tuned lead-generation machine is one of the aspects of a successful, scalable, and profitable business. And it's the one model that is truly scalable and sustainable.

Don't buy leads and data, generate them.

This page intentionally left blank.

Learn more @ aaronopfell.com

NOTES

i "Internet Usage Statistics: The Internet Big Picture," *Internet World Stats*,
http://www.internetworldstats.com/stats.htm

ii Interactive Advertising Bureau, "IAB Internet Advertising Revenue Report,"
http://www.iab.net/research/industry_data_and_land scape/adrevenuereport

iii "Are Young People Watching Less TV?" *MarketingCharts*,
http://www.marketingcharts.com/wp/television/are -young-people-watching-less-tv-24817/

iv Ernesto Van Der Sar, "Music Piracy Continues to Decline Thanks to Spotify," *TorrentFreak*,
http://torrentfreak.com/music-piracy-continues-to- decline-thanks-to-spotify-110928/

v Russell Adams, "Papers Put Faith in Paywalls," *The Wall Street Journal*,
http://online.wsj.com/news/articles/SB100014240529 70203833004577251822631536422

vi UserExperienceWorks, "A Magazine Is an iPad That Does Not Work," *YouTube*,
http://www.youtube.com/watch?v=aXV-yaFmQNk

vii "Uncovering Demographic Differences in Tablet Activities," *eMarketer*,
http://www.emarketer.com/Article/Uncovering- Demographic-Differences-Tablet-Activities/1009244

viii Aaron Smith, "Smartphone Ownership 2013," *Pew Research Internet Project*,

http://www.pewinternet.org/2013/06/05/smartphon
e-ownership-2013/

ix Courtney Boyd Myers, "Global Spam Filtering Arrives for
Google Voice," *The Next Web*,
http://thenextweb.com/google/2011/07/12/global-
spam-filtering-arrives-for-google-voice/

x "Direct Mail Tops Email for Response Rates; Costs per Lead
Similar," *MarketingCharts*,
http://www.marketingcharts.com/wp/traditional/di
rect-mail-tops-email-for-response-rates-costs-per-
lead-similar-22395/

xi "Google Algorithm Change History," *Moz*,
http://moz.com/google-algorithm-change

xii Matt Cutts, "Another Step to Reward High-Quality Sites,"
Google Inside Search,
http://insidesearch.blogspot.com/2012/04/another-
step-to-reward-high-quality.html

xiii "Link Schemes," *Google Webmaster Tools*,
https://support.google.com/webmasters/answer/663
56

xiv Ryan Holiday, *Trust Me, I'm Lying: Confessions of a Media
Manipulator*, New York: Portfolio 2012

xv "Usage Statistics and Market Share of WordPress for
Websites," *W3Techs: Web Technology Surveys*,
http://w3techs.com/technologies/details/cm-
wordpress/all/all

xvi Jon Henshaw, "The Problem with Infographics and SEO
(and How to Fix It)," *Squawk*,
http://squawk.im/seo/infographics-and-seo/

xvii Steve Jobs, "Thoughts on Flash," Apple website,

http://www.apple.com/hotnews/thoughts-on-flash/

xviii Mike Isaac, "About Those Google+ User Numbers," *All Things D*, http://allthingsd.com/20131031/about-those-google-user-numbers/

xix Richard Hanna, Andrew Rohm, and Victoria L. Crittenden, "We're All Connected: The Power of the Social Media Ecosystem," *Business Horizons*, May-June 2011, http://topgan.cce.unsyiah.ac.id/Were%20all%20connected%20The%20power%20of%20the%20social%20media%20ecosystem.pdf

xx Julie Bort, "How Many Web Sites Are There?" *Business Insider*, http://www.businessinsider.com/how-many-web-sites-are-are-there-2012-3

xxi Eric Jaffe, "These Scientists Studied Why Internet Stories Go Viral. You Won't Believe What They Found," *Fast Company*, http://www.fastcodesign.com/3024276/evidence/these-scientists-studied-why-internet-stories-go-viral-you-wont-believe-what-they-f

xxii John Patrick Pullen, "How a Dollar Shave Club's Ad Went Viral," *Entrepreneur*, http://www.entrepreneur.com/article/224282

xxiii Tom Clark, "Top 10 Viral Marketing Disasters – Part 2 (5-1)," *Lakestar McCann Blog*, http://www.lakestarmccann.com/blog/general-news/viral-marketing/top-10-viral-marketing-disasters-part-2-5-1/

xxiv Chris Wilson, "Will My Video Get 1 Million Views on YouTube?" *Slate*, http://www.slate.com/articles/technology/webhead

/2009/07/will_my_video_get_1_million_views_on_youtub
e.html

xxv Laura Stampler, "Why Zappos Sees Sponsored Posts on
Facebook as 'A Necessary Evil,'" *Business Insider*,
http://www.businessinsider.com/zappos-on-
facebook-and-social-media-2013-2

xxvi Sebastian Haley, "Ocean Marketing: How to Self-Destruct
Your Company with Just a Few Measly Emails
[update]," *VentureBeat*,
http://venturebeat.com/2011/12/27/ocean-
marketing-how-to-self-destruct-your-company-
with-just-a-few-measly-emails/2/

xxvii George Anders, "Today I Learned: Reddit Could be
Worth $240 Million," *Forbes*,
http://www.forbes.com/sites/georgeanders/2012/10/
31/what-is-reddit-worth/

xxviii Brittany Darwell, "Facebook Conversion Tracking Goes
Live for All Ad Accounts," MediaBistro *Inside
Facebook*,
http://www.insidefacebook.com/2013/01/22/faceboo
k-conversion-tracking-goes-live-for-all-ad-accounts/

xxix Jim Edwards, "This LinkedIn Deck Shows the ROI for 8 of
Its Biggest Ad Clients," *Business Insider*,
http://www.businessinsider.com/see-8-of-the-most-
effective-ad-campaigns-that-ran-on-linkedin-2012-
8?op=1

xxx "InMail: The Most Credible Way to Message Anyone on
Linked In," LinkedIn website,
http://www.linkedin.com/static?key=about_inmail

xxxi "Native Advertising," Sharethrough website,
http://www.sharethrough.com/nativeadvertising/

xxxii "CAN-SPAM Act: A Compliance Guide for Business," Bureau of Consumer Protection *Business Center*, http://www.business.ftc.gov/documents/bus61-can-spam-act-compliance-guide-business

xxxiii "Google Annual Search Statistics," *Statistic Brain*, http://www.statisticbrain.com/google-searches/

xxxiv "HTTP Cookie," *Wikipedia*, http://en.wikipedia.org/wiki/HTTP_cookie

xxxv Do Not Track Me Online Act of 2011, H.R. 654,112th Congress, http://www.gpo.gov/fdsys/pkg/BILLS-112hr654ih/pdf/BILLS-112hr654ih.pdf

xxxvi Katy Bachman, "Markey, Barton Bring Back Do Not Track Kids Bill," *Adweek*, http://www.adweek.com/news/technology/markey-barton-bring-back-do-not-track-kids-bill-153860

xxxvii "When You Search Google," Don't Track Us website, http://donttrack.us/

xxxviii Amanda Kelly, "AdWords Click Measurements Accredited by MRC," *Google Inside AdWords*, http://adwords.blogspot.com/2009/06/adwords-click-measurements-accredited.html